True Murder Stories

———— ❧❦❧ ————

Vicious Cold Case Killers, True Crime, Serial Killers and True Murder Stories of Violent Criminals

Brody Clayton

Table of Contents

Like FREE books?

Would you like them delivered to you every week?

Do you like non-fiction books on a huge range of different topics?

We send out FREE e-books every week so we can share our books with the world!

We have FREE books every week on AMAZON that we send to our email list.

So if you want in, then visit the link at the end of this book to sign up and sit back and wait for new books to be sent straight to your inbox!

Book Description

This book is a shocking collection of the world's most gruesome murder incidents from all over the world. A treasure cove for any crime and murder enthusiast, these stories will definitely have you locking your doors at night.

With this book you'll get a deep insight into some of the world's most evil men and women, who managed to strike terror into the hearts of men and sprayed the pages of history with blood.

Well some of them were punished for their doings; others managed to evade detection, and hid themselves, only to be remembered in time as some of the most prolific killers the world has seen. To understand the perversions of such a twisted mind may in fact seem like quite a hard task indeed, however one can only try to see the world through the bloody lens that these criminals do.

Motives, methods and the killer's point of view are all quite enthralling to read, even more so when the you place yourself in the victim's shoes.

However, it is important to remember that all the stories in this book are true stories, and not just a figment of a writer's imagination...

Introduction

Since the beginning of time we have seen instances when the sanctity of human life has been tarnished and blood has been spilt. The Biblical story of Cain and Abel is itself a testament to the fact that Mankind can be open to horrible acts of cruelty against each other and also against one's own soul.

Most of these instances have been fueled by human motive such as revenge or jealousy. But sometimes, through the course of history, some people have violated this sanctity and derived pleasure out of the cruelty of their ways.

They have shown absolutely no moral repulsion for their actions, and thus become one of the most famous people on Earth, for their ruthless spillage of blood, that left them completely devoid of all human compassion.

In other scenarios, they truly believed their actions would bring some good, and their delusions led them to commit horrifying sins. While some famous criminals such as Ted Bundy and Jeffrey Dahmer are well known by any criminal enthusiast, there are many more violent criminals out there who committed crimes much more heinous, and in fact managed to get away with it and were never even found.

Introduction

This book explores the stories of just a few, in an effort to understand the workings of their mind, and the true psychology of a killer...

The information herein is offered for informational purposes solely, and is universal as so. The presentation of the information is without contract or any type of guarantee assurance.

The trademarks that are used are without any consent, and the publication of the trademark is without permission or backing by the trademark owner. All trademarks and brands within this book are for clarifying purposes only and are the owned by the owners themselves, not affiliated with this document.

CHAPTER 1:

Peter Kurten:
The 'Vampire' Killer

The term 'vampire' may make you think of a mystical creature from old childhood stories, of misty nights and dark allies, and most importantly, the idea that they only exist in movies and books.

However, one of the most notorious vampires in history was not at all part of any ancient mythical story. The vicious crimes that this man committed occurred in Germany, making him popularly known as "The Vampire of Dusseldorf.".

The night of May 25th, 1913 a shadow skulked among the darkness, stealing from various bars and inns in Cologne-Mulheim, evading detection. He crept from room to room, trying door after door but alas, he couldn't find anything worth stealing. He entered a room and found a young eight year old girl fast asleep in bed.

He grabbed the child's head, and started to strangle her. He did so for about one and a half minutes, all the while the child having woken up, she struggled but soon gave in to the monster attacking her and fell unconscious. He assaulted her, but even that wasn't enough. He paused, unsure of how to proceed but then a new idea gave birth in the evil recesses of his twisted mind.

He extracted a pen-knife, though small but equally sharp and held the cold edge against the girl's throat. In one quick motion, he grabbed her head and slit her throat, paying attention to the sound of her blood spurting from her neck and dripping down to the floor. This very sound enthralled him, and he was drawn hypnotically to the blood that coated everything.

Having done the deed, the monster locked the door, and returned back to his home in Dusseldorf. His name was Peter Kurten.

The next day, Peter returned back to the scene, and found himself sitting leisurely at a café which was right across from where he had killed his victim. People around him were talking about the murder, and instead of striking some worry or fear of discovery in his heart, he felt proud of his doing. This narration of the events that transpired was told by Kurten himself in court, without any emotion or remorse whatsoever.

The child's name had been Christine Klein, and when her body was found it was pale and her tongue was badly bitten. On her neck, two wounds were visible. One was shallow, suggesting that it had been made by a single stroke, the second one however, was much deeper, about nine centimetres.

This wound had been made by four separate movements. In the same room, a handkerchief was found, with initials 'P.K' on it, however it was assumed that it belonged to the child's father Peter Klein. The suspicion of this brutal murder fell on the girl's uncle Otto, and while Kurten sat in the café the next day listening to the details of the murder he had committed and how Otto was suspected, the killer inside him came alive.

He was safe from any suspicion, and his killer impulses had been awakened. However, it was not until a couple of years later that he unleashed his full malice upon his poor victims.

The shaping of a killer:

Without any doubt, Peter Kurten had a violent upbringing, and his sadistic tendencies became quite apparent even as a child. Subject to frequent assault by his drunk, abusive father he too developed cruel impulses and soon enough this became apparent in his behavior. At the age of nine, he became friends with a dogcatcher and started working for him, torturing the poor animals.

He enjoyed torturing all the various animals he managed to round up, and he progressed from dogs to goats, sheep and even pigs. The sight of blood attracted him, and he derived great pleasure by cutting of a swan or goose's head and drinking the blood that spurted out of the beheaded animal. Soon however, his victims switched from animals to human beings.

Kurten drowned two of his playmates while they were playing in the river Rhine. He first drowned one of them, but when the other friend jumped to save the first one, Kurten pushed him under the raft they were playing on and kept him down until he eventually drowned.

However, these deaths didn't excite him much. They were too clean, too mundane for his liking. He started pursuing excitement by stealing and other various crimes, which included beating up prostitutes. As his blood lust increased however, he eventually ended up planning his first, thought out murder.

Luckily, for the first victim, his first attack was a failure. He planned and attacked a girl in a park and ended up leaving her for dead. The girl however, survived and crawled away, too stigmatized to even go to the police. However, this was only the first in the series of murders to follow; the Vampire of Dusseldorf had only started his spree.

The savagery continues:

After his first murder of Christine Klein, Kurten spent most of World War One in jail, to be exact after he deserted the army for which he had been called up for service for. He was freed and then ended up in jail again due to fraud.

Finally he was released in 1921, and for the next four years it seemed that the monster had finally come under control. He got married, and got a job in a factory. He was well-dressed and well-spoken and thus it was alarming when in 1925, he reverted back to his old form.

Peter went back to visit Dusseldorf as he had been settled in Altenburg for quite some time, and on returning back to his old city his vicious criminal side revived. He started carrying out arson attacks, petty crimes, and also started attacking various strangers on the street only because the sight of their blood was so hypnotic to him.

In 1929 however, the Vampire of Dusseldorf evolved into his full fledged form and unleashed horrors on to the residents of the city.

The Dusseldorf police became aware of a body that was discovered under a hedge on the ninth of February in 1929. The victim was only eight years of age, and her name was Rosa. She had been stabbed a total of about thirteen times, and her body was also partially burnt and her body was doused in petrol.

Just a couple of days before this incident came to surface, Kurten grabbed a woman by the name of Frau Kuhn and proceeded to stab her repeatedly, and only ran off after he had succeeded in stabbing her twenty four times. However, just the act of attacking her wasn't enough for Kurten, and he got sick pleasure out of going back to the scene of his crime.

Five days after the murder of Rosa, a 45 year old mechanic was found dead on a deserted road. The man, whose name was Scheer had 22 stab wounds, including wounds to the head. Again, Kurten returned to where he had committed his crime, and was bold enough to have a conversation with one of the detectives on site.

This only further emphasized how dangerous Kurten had really become. His criminal psyche had evolved way past the point that he had any fear left of being discovered. His actions were purely fuelled by blood lust and sadism.

In the month of August, Kurten carried out a series of stabbings and strangulations that had the police more alarmed than ever. Three people were stabbed as they walked home one night, on 21st August. The victims, all random were each wished a 'Good Evening' before Kurten stabbed them in their back and ribs. From here onwards the crimes only escalated in intensity.

CHAPTER 1: Peter Kurten: the 'Vampire' Killer

On the twenty third of August in the town of Flehe an annual fair had been organized. Hundreds of people were attending the event and among them, were two sisters, Gertrude and Louise who were 5 and 14 respectively.

The two foster sisters decided to walk home that night at around ten thirty, except as they left they noticed that someone quietly walked out from the trees and was now on the footpath behind them. The man kindly asked the elder sister to get him some cigarettes. He promised to keep an eye on the little girl, and Louise ran off taking the man's money to do as he had said.

Meanwhile the man picked up Gertrude and while she was in his arms he strangled the child, and then proceeded to cut her throat. Louise came back with his cigarettes, only to find her sister gone, and she soon met the same fate.

The man dragged her away and strangled her too, except he proceeded to also decapitate her, and thus ended the lives of Gertrude and Louise at the hands of Peter Kurten.

This was not all. These attacks were followed by attacks just as cruel. A servant girl by the name of Gertrude was stabbed; however she survived and managed to give a very vivid description of the man who attacked her. Later, a young girl was raped and then killed in September, and in October another girl was beaten to death. Her name was Elizabeth. In December there were attacks of two more women.

Understandably, the entire city of Dusseldorf was in a state of panic. There was mass hysteria that only increased as the bodies piled up. In November a young 5 year old was kidnapped and a letter showed up at a newspaper, which gave directions to her body. The instructions led straight to her.

She had been stabbed about 35 times. The panic that had managed to spread through the city was comparable to the fear that was rampant in England due to Jack the Ripper. There was a huge manhunt going on, the police were on high alert yet there was no clue that was leading them to the killer.

Unphased by the public outcry, Kurten continued with his activities, and Dusseldorf held its breath in fear, as the 'Vampire' was still very active and the murder count kept increasing.

The Arrest of the Vampire Killer:

The events that led up to the final capture of the Vampire Killer happened more or less by accident. On the 14th may in the year 1930, a servant by the name of Maria left her home town Koln and started traveling to Dusseldorf to get work.

While at the platform at the station of Dusseldorf, she met a man who volunteered to take her to a girl's hostel that was close by. However, the man started taking her towards a park, and knowing the murder scare that was rampant, she refused to go ahead with him.

The man however was persistent and they started arguing. A second gentleman entered the situation and asked if he may be of assistance. Seeing this, the first man left, and Maria was left with her savior, Peter Kurten.

Kurten led her to the woods, and there he assaulted her, however he did something this time he had never done before, he let her go. Kurten had assumed that Maria would never be able to find her way back to his house that he had tried to lure her to originally. However he was wrong.

CHAPTER 1: Peter Kurten: the 'Vampire' Killer

Maria remembered the street and even though she was too intimidated and embarrassed to go to the police she narrated the entire incident to a friend in a letter. Call it fate, but the letter didn't reach the right address, and the recipient opened it, looked at the contents of the letter and promptly involved the police.

Maria was traced and questioned after which she led them to Peter Kurten's house. Peter, who by now had become aware that he would soon be captured, went and confessed to his wife who then told the police. The day that Kurten was finally taken into custody, four officers with guns surrounded him, when he finally appeared, he smiled, completely at ease and informed the officers that they had no reason to be afraid of him.

Once in custody, Kurten was quite candid about his murders and narrated with honesty all his offences. It was pretty apparent that Peter enjoyed the look of horror that his stories would cause in the people listening to them.

Eventually, the man was charged with murder and was found guilty. He was to be given the death sentence at the guillotine and instead of being afraid he very eagerly asked his psychiatrist whether he would still be able to hear his blood spurt out from his neck as it is cut off, even if just for a brief minute. The thought of this appealed to him greatly, and he said that the pleasure that it would give him would surpass all pleasures he had ever felt.

And thus ended the story of the Vampire of Dusseldorf, whose terror spread far and wide and whose victims died painful, vicious deaths. But while his bloody sprees had finally come to an end, many more sprang up to take his place.

CHAPTER 2:

Cold Cases – The Zodiac Killer

One of the most well-known cases in the criminal enthusiast community is the Zodiac Killer. It is one case that has baffled detectives for years and every amateur sleuth tries to go over all the facts of the case and crack the case on their own.

The enigmatic killer, who named himself the zodiac, was a serial killer who was very active in the 1960s and 70s. He was based in California, and while his confirmed kills are only five, he is thought to have killed at least 37 people.

The Zodiac had a very narcissistic personality, and he reveled in the attention that his murders got. He wanted for himself to be known by taunting the detectives on his case at the same time, and thus sent letters to the print media and the police daring them to figure his identity out.

It is speculated that he did eventually want people to know who he was, but he was also interested in finding out whether someone could outsmart him and figure it out instead. However, how exactly did his killing spree start?

It is widely believed that his first victim was a college student who went by the name of Cheri Jo Bates, and she was killed right outside her school's library in 1966. While some people claim to have seen a white man driving an old car around that place sometime around the time she was murdered, the police also found a watch at the scene of the crime.

After a month had gone by, a letter was received by a newspaper, and it was said to have been sent by the killer himself. Many months afterwards, letters started being received by not just the media but also the police, and sadly Bates' father too. All of the letters had the exact same message on them:

"Bates had to die. There will be more."

In 1968, the Zodiac followed through on his ominous message. A young teenage couple were out together and had their car parked when David Faraday was shot in the head, while he was still inside the car. Alarmed, Betty Lou got outside the vehicle but before she could escape she was targeted and shot five times in the back.

In 1969, another couple was attacked by the Zodiac Killer. Mike and Darlene were parked when a second car came and parked right beside them. The killer then exited his car and walked to the passenger door of the couple's car. He shined a flashlight into their eyes and then shot them five times.

The Zodiac then started to walk away from the scene, but then he heard Mike moaning and walked back to the two, shooting them two more times and then driving away.

The very next day, the police got a call from a man who claimed that he was responsible. He even claimed responsibility for the first attack. That was when the police realized the gravity of the situation: they were dealing with a serial killer.

Shortly afterwards, three newspapers received letters that were supposedly sent by the killer himself. The three letters that were sent to each newspaper respectively, were pretty much the same, and took credit for the murders. Here is the interesting part however.

Each letter had a cryptogram, which was one-third of the whole cryptogram. By combining the three letters and deciphering the whole cryptogram, the killer promised that his identity could be uncovered.

All three parts of the message were eventually decoded and published. This was when the Zodiac started garnering public attention. On August 7th, one of the newspapers received a second letter. There was a difference in the tone of this letter.

He directly addressed the editor and for the first time ever, he used the term "Zodiac" as his identification. The letter gave more details about the murders that had not been released to the public, thus this confirmed that the letters were in fact from the killer.

According to the cryptogram, the Zodiac was killing his victims and actually choosing them to be his slaves. He claimed that he would be re-born in Paradise, and all these people would be his slaves. He didn't want to reveal his identity for this very reason, because it would cause him to either have to stop or slow down the process.

The Attacks Continue:

It was clear that the Zodiac killer had no intention of slowing down. In September of the same year, he carried out his next attack. Two young students, Bryan Hartnell and Cecilia Shepard were at Lake Berryessa when they were attacked.

However this time the Zodiac was much more violent. He didn't choose a gun as his murder weapon this time, instead he chose a knife.

After tying the two of them up, he stabbed them again and again, and then drew his signature symbol (cross/circle) on Hartnell's car door, even including the date of the previous murder he committed. As the two screamed when they were stabbed, this drew the attention of some people fishing nearby who found them and then called the police.

From the description by Shepard, who eventually succumbed to her wounds, a description of her attacker could finally be made. They described him as a white, heavyset male who was in his twenties or at the most thirties. He had brown hair which was short, and wore thick glasses. However, while he attacked them he wore a very large hood.

After this attack, The Zodiac again called to report his crime, as was his habit. Two weeks later, the Killer shot his next victim in October. This time, there were three witnesses to the crime when a taxi driver was shot in the head. The Zodiac then took his keys and also his wallet, and also a piece of the victim's clothing.

Yet, despite them seeing the Zodiac, they were still unable to catch him, and once again he evaded arrest. A few days letter, another letter was received which reported his latest murder but also threatened to kill children in a school bus. Luckily, he didn't follow through on that plan.

More cryptic messages:

The Zodiac loved highlighting his work, and thus with his latest later he also sent the piece of the taxi driver's shirt as proof of his deed. In November, another coded message was received by the Zodiac. Unfortunately, no one has been able to crack it to this day.

He continued to send more letters, taunting the police, deriving pleasure out of their inability to track him down. Meanwhile the Zodiac continued his attacks, even trying to kidnap and kill a pregnant women and her daughter but failing as they escaped.

What baffled detectives and everyone else involved in the case the most however, were the various coded letters and various ominous messages they kept receiving. He even sent ciphers that if decoded, would give his name, yet they weren't cracked. With every new victim or plan he executed, he sent a note with a score of his deeds.

(Cross-circle symbol) =12 SFPD=0

The Zodiac Killer's Symbol

This was to rile up the police department due to their persistent failure to find him. He even sent threats to a reporter who was covering the case, who received a Halloween card with a note that said he was doomed.

It was obvious that through these tactics the Zodiac was not only able to instill paranoia among the people of California but also greatly intrigue those trying to discover his identity.

CHAPTER 2: Cold Cases – The Zodiac Killer

The last letter by the Zodiac was received in 1974. It had a symbol on it that has still gone unexplained, but more importantly, the Zodiac left his last score on the note:

(Zodiac symbol) =37, SFPD =0

The case of the Zodiac Killer remained open for many years until it was finally closed. It may have been re-opened at a further date but to no avail. Some of the detectives on the case spent their whole lives working on it, yet to this day no one knows who the Zodiac Killer was. There were many suspects, yet none could be specifically tied to the murder.

All that we know for sure is this; the Zodiac Killer was highly intelligent, and his acts of violence were merely a game he was playing with the police. His messages, codes, and letters are available to this day, yet he still remains unknown, maybe even still alive, and proud of the blood that he spilt in his wake.

CHAPTER 3:

Cold Cases –
The Black Dahlia Murder

One of the most gruesome unsolved murders to this date is The Black Dahlia Murder. It may have been just one case, but the murder itself was so violent and savage, that it gained a lot of popularity at the time with almost every newspaper covering the story.

No one was able to track the killer or reveal his identity, yet this case is one that has been speculated over and talked about for years. Every time a new movie comes out in reference to this murder, more people line up claiming somebody they know is the real murderer.

The name of the victim was Elizabeth Short, but after her murder she became known more popularly as The Black Dahlia, a name given to her by the various newspapers covering her story.

Elizabeth Short – Black Dahlia

The body was discovered on the fifteenth of January, in 1947. While walking in Liemert Park in Los Angeles, a woman saw what she thought was a discarded mannequin from a store that was lying among the weeds, partially hidden from plain view. As she got closer she realized to her horror that what she had before her was no mannequin, it was a human being.

When the police arrived, the scene that greeted them was awful. In the weeds, lay the body of a woman. She was naked but the upper half of her body was completely separated from the lower half. The body had been severely disfigured and mutilated, so much so that the face had been cut in half, with the cut running from both ends of her mouth.

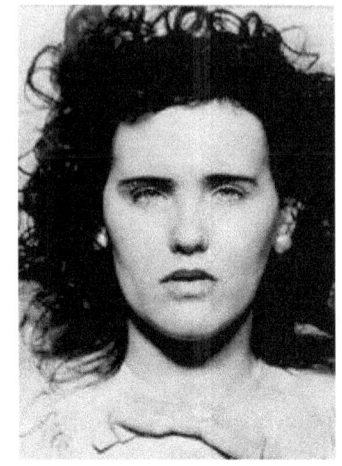

If that wasn't enough, her body had been cut and slashed extensively, especially on her breasts and face. Her body had been carefully laid down in the grass, with the arms posed above her head. There were also additional marks on her body.

Her legs and ankles had different rope burns, and her legs were laying spread at a wide angle. Curiously, there were some initials that were marked into one thigh. It read, 'BD.'

Since there was no blood that was apparent around the body even around the scene of the crime thus it became apparent that the murder of the young girl has not been committed here. She had in fact been killed at some other place but her body laid out to get the public's attention. The killer had made sure to drain the body of the last drop of blood. Elizabeth was only twenty two years old at the time.

There was no murder weapon, no forensic evidence, not even footprints. There was nothing apart from the remains of the poor girl that could help determine who carried out the atrocity. Her hair also wet, and the young girl who wanted to someday become an actress, had had her dreams cut short by someone who was nothing less than an animal.

By the time additional police arrived at the crime scene, a hoard of photographers and newspaper reporters had also already started to swarm to the site much to the annoyance of the investigators Harry and Finis.

The two investigators were very experienced and thus were given this case to handle, to help get to the bottom of it ASAP. Yet for months it was nothing but a huge media fiasco. The murder was front page news and hundreds of people confessed to the murder, hoping to get their fifteen minutes of fame.

Since there was no substantial evidence found at the crime scene, and with no concrete evidence that helped point to the primary scene of the crime, the investigators had no choice but to study in detail the body itself. It was concluded that the body had probably been cut in half with either an electric saw or a butcher's knife.

If that wasn't vicious enough, the injuries sustained by her were even more gruesome. Her face had been slashed from ear to ear, making it look like the she was smiling even in death. Even though there was no indication that she had in fact between strangulated to death, the bruising on her battered body was extensive.

There were marks on her neck as well as her head. Her upper lip also had multiple cuts. There were more scratches and cuts on her arms, chest and torso. Even more horrifically, On examination it was discovered that there was a piece of skin from her thigh that was missing.

Elizabeth had had a tattoo of a rose on her thigh, and that piece of skin had been removed and it was later discovered inside her body, shoved up her vaginal orifice. What the reason behind this especially brutal act, baffled investigators.

It was very clear though that she had been tortured not just before she passed away but her body had also been abused once she was already dead. The cause of her death was determined to be the massive injuries she had to her neck and also her head. The extent of hurt caused to her body showed that there was definite overkill when it came to this murder.

Whoever had taken her life did so in an inexplicable fit of anger and rage, and it was by someone who had been close to her. Another possibility was that she was a victim of a psychopath, however if this was the case, the brutality and sever mutilation that her body underwent mean that this had to be a seasoned psychopath who had spent years hunting down victims and building on their madness. The idea that this might have been a serial killer was even more terrifying.

A very detailed investigation was carried out, with many false reports and dead ends. There was no hard evidence that could be used, no solid leads, and eventually the case was just left cold. From time to time, the case may have been opened again, but the lack of any solid leads forced investigators to ignore the case altogether, and leave Elizabeth Short without any justice.

THEORY:

Cleveland Torso Killer

One psychopath serial killer, who some people believed was linked to this murder, was the Cleveland Torso Killer. He was a man who murdered in Ohio, and he would completely dismember the people he preyed on in some way.

The level of brutality displayed in the Black Dahlia murder perfectly matched his handiwork. However the Cleveland Torso Killer disappeared and was never caught. It was possible however, that he committed one more crime in California and then just disappeared.

There were other various suspects tied to the case, but it was all inconclusive. The brutal murder has been immortalized in books and movies, as the life of a girl whose life was cut too short by the hands of a monster.

CHAPTER 4:

Leonarda Cianciulli –
The Soap Maker of Correggio

While men are most often accused of the bulk of cruel, brutal murders, women too have played their fair share in the history of violent crime. One such example is of Leonarda Cianculli who carried out her crimes in the city of Correggio in Italy. While she may have had only three victims, the brutal treatment these victims went through set this woman apart from all the rest.

Leonarda Cianciulli was a very capable woman who was also very resourceful, and in the 1930s when times were tough, she knew how to make do with what little she had been provided with.

She had been married to her husband, Raffaele in 1914. Many years before, a fortune teller had told her that when she marries and has children, all of them will die in succession. Call it the doing of some supernatural forces, but when she did get married finally she got pregnant seventeen times out of which she had miscarriages three times.

Ten of her children all passed away when they were quite young, thus she was extremely protective of the four children that she had left. She would often consult with psychics and other fortune tellers as she lived in constant fear that they too would be taken away from her according to the gypsy's prophecy.

Around this same time period, the eldest child born to her; Giuseppe, was finally old enough to be called to fight in the war. He was her most favourite, and the idea that she might end up losing him in the war effort was something she just could not deal with. That was when she felt that she must appeal to some supernatural power and employ occult techniques to help preserve her son's life and keep her children close to her.

This was when she came up with the idea of what she had to do. By taking the life of another person, she would maintain the balance of nature and appease the higher powers. This way her child would not be separated from her. Having pondered over this for quite some time she decided that this was what she absolutely had to do.

Having built her life in this city she had come to know a lot of people and was generally a well respected lady. However she understood that she must sacrifice some of her relationships for a son and that was a price she was willing to pay quite eagerly.

She planned to take the life of her neighbor, Faustina Setti. Faustina had wanted a husband for a very long time and it was no secret that she was looking for a match for herself. Faustine had actually sought out Leonarda for help, as she also acted as a match maker for the local community. Leonarda had told her that she would try her best to set her up with a suitable match, and now was the perfect time for her to act.

Leonarda got in touch with Faustina, and told her that she had succeeded in finding a good man for her, however he lived very far away and thus Faustina would have to travel to meet him.

She advised Faustina, to not tell people that she was planning to leave to prevent senseless gossip, but she should write letters that can be dispatched much later so her close relations would know that she is doing well. Having taken care of any loose ends, Leonarda got down to business.

She served her friend wine that was drugged, and once her victim was unconscious, she killed her with an axe. However that was not enough for Leonarda. Instead of finding a way to dispose of the body she had another idea. She took the body and dragged it away and hid it in a closet. Then, using the same axe again, she cut the body up into nine parts precisely, and meticulously gathered all the blood that was spilt in a basin.

Having done this, she put pieces of the dead body, along with caustic soda, together and once it had all dissolved she poured the dark mixture in a septic tank nearby. The blood however, she had other plans for. She dried the blood in her oven and incorporated the crunchy blood into her tea cakes, which she then served to not only guests but even ate herself. She was very proud of her accomplishment and for a while she was very content with how things had turned out.

However, the tea cakes didn't last for long, and her old fears set in all over again. She felt it was now time to renew her sacrifice, maybe the fates needed to be appeased all over again. Or maybe the blood lust that had formed inside her just could no longer be contained. Whatever the reasons, it became clear to her that she needed a second victim.

Her next victim was also another neighbor of hers, by the name of Francesca. She too had come to Leonarda for help for a job position she desperately wanted. As she did the first time, she told Francesca that a job was available for her, but that too was in a place quite far from her current residence, at a school for girls.

Leonarda advised that it would be better if she didn't tell people about her job to prevent jealousy from others, and it would be best if she just told those close to her that she was going away for a while.

And as it happened the first time she killed her with an axe, cut up her body and added it in a pot with caustic soda. This time however instead of discarding the mixture, she ended up making soap, which she then gladly gave to her neighbors and acquaintances who were absolutely delighted with her gift. The blood she used to make some more teacakes.

Thus apart from sacrificing these women in lieu of her son's life, she started quite a nice business, involving soap and teacakes.

Leonarda also trapped a third victim the same way. She was extremely satisfied with her third sacrifice, and while her victim Virginia was being used to make soap, she added cologne to this batch. She made an observation that Virginia made for a much better quality of soap and even the tea cakes were so much more delicious.

Unfortunately, Virginia's family members were not as gullible as the rest. Her sister in law was especially suspicious of Leonarda, as she saw Virginia enter Leonarda's home the last time she saw her.

Investigations began and soon suspicions turned to evidence and eventually Leonarda confessed to her doing. She felt that had she hidden her deeds, that it might reverse the result of the sacrifices she had made.

Well the murders that Leonarda committed may sound a little comical; they were in fact a sign of how brutal the human mind can play itself out to be. Leonarda was sent to jail for about thirty years or so, but whether she felt any remorse over her doings, that cannot be said. After all, she managed to save her son's life, and to her that was what was most important.

CHAPTER 5:

David Parker Ray – The Toy Box Killer

O n the afternoon of March 22, in the year 1999 a young woman fled down a deserted road, running to save her life. She was completed naked and the dirt road was hurting her feet, but she could not focus on any of that as she sped down the road to run from the monster she was trying to get away from.

Cynthia ran as hard as she could through the New Mexico desert. A woman was driving by, but when she saw Cynthia she freaked out and raced off after locking her doors. Cynthia didn't really understand what she looked like at that moment.

There was blood that was seeping through an injury to her head, while a collar made of metal was around her neck. There was also a chain attached to it that was dangling behind her. Another car passed by, but the end was the same.

Cynthia felt absolutely devastated. She did come along various trailers along the way but they seemed empty, and she was so scared of what was following her she did not have it in her to stop even for a minute in case she was being followed.

Finally she saw a home that looked well-maintained and thanked God that the door was open. Without a second thought she raced inside the home and locked the door behind her only to find a very shocked woman staring at her. She begged the woman to help her, and once the lady realized how badly injured Cynthia was, she started to help her.

Cynthia's hair was matted with blood and there was blood and bruising all over her abused body. The owner called the police, meanwhile allowing Cynthia to cover herself with some clothing that she provided.

Cynthia could not believe how far away from home she was. More importantly she could not believe that she had managed to survive. She tried her best to tell the officers what exactly had happened to her, but how could she put her whole ordeal into words? She told them that she was kidnapped and her abductor along with a female accomplice kept her hostage and subjected her to torture with various instruments.

Her kidnapper had left just a while before, and the female accomplice was responsible for Cynthia. However the minute she left the room, Cynthia lunged for the keys that hung not very far from her and set herself free from the pole that she was chained to.

She saw a phone and tried to call the police as soon as possible, but just at that moment the woman returned again, and seeing Cynthia attempting to escape she threw a lamp that struck Cynthia's head. Cynthia fell, but grabbed an ice pick that had been used to torture her and swung it at the woman who backed off.

Taking her chances Cynthia raced out the door, without her clothes or anything else apart from the desperation to escape from the Hell that she had been trapped in.

Cynthia tried her best to tell the police where her abductors had been holding her, but the police were already following the call that Cynthia had tried to make earlier. Meanwhile, Cynthia went to a hospital and the doctors were appalled at the abuse that she had gone through. There were bruises and burn marks all over her body, and it became apparent that there was a sadistic kidnapper on the loose.

Cynthia met her abductor while working as a prostitute. Her kidnapper, Ray offered her money for her services and she got into his car with him, except she came across Ray's girlfriend. Even though at this point Cynthia did feel quite uncomfortable, Ray pulled out a police badge and informed her she was being arrested.

However, soon the two of them tied her up and gagged her, and this was when it became apparent to her that she was not under arrest, this was an abduction. They put a metal collar on her neck and put tape on her mouth to prevent her from speaking. Cynthia felt like it had been hours since they had been driving and hopelessness started to set in.

They took her to a trailer and chained her. It then became apparent to her what was going to become of her. They forced her to watch a video that told her of all the torture she would have to go through. She was to be treated as a sex slave, and would be compliant to all of Ray's wishes just like the other women before her who had eventually been killed.

David and his girlfriend Cindy tortured her endlessly, whipping her, threatening her, hanging her from the ceiling. They used different instruments to cause her pain until she couldn't take it anymore.

In response to Cynthia's interrupted call to 911, David Ray and Cindy were both located and taken into custody. Soon a warrant was obtained and their house searched, but no one could have imagined what they were about to find.

The Toy Box:

Just like Cynthia said, they found a broken lamp as well as a gun. They also found the badge that Ray had used to fool Cynthia. Cynthia's clothes were there too, along with various instruments and the audiotape that Cynthia was made to listen to.

The worst however, was their discovery of what Ray called his 'toy box.' They found a smaller trailer, and it was also called the 'secure room.' The entire space was wholly for the practice of torture on Ray's victims. He had intricate plans and designs, drawn of all that he planned to do to his victim.

Alongside this he had a wide array of surgical instruments to cause pain to his subject and follow through on his grand plans. His toy box also contained manuals on the female body, and different sexual equipment as well. He had even built an electrical device specifically designed to cause pain on the woman he tortured. He had videos of himself torturing his previous victims while they screamed in pain.

Ray had a monitor that he placed in view of his victims so they could see exactly what he was doing to them. His entire toy box was his sadistic heaven filled will images of him torturing his previous victims.

He had even created his own manual on how to handle a slave. He talked about subjecting the slave to torture both physically and psychologically, and also reinforced this with additional verbal abuse. He even had detailed methods to brainwash someone and various tactics to scare them.

With all the evidence gathered against them, finally, Ray and his girlfriend were arrested however even then there were chances that they could walk free. However, soon other victims began to surface.

Another woman, by the name of Angelica came forward and gave a detailed description of the torture she had been put through.

She had come to their house only looking for cake mix, but instead they kidnapped her and tortured her for four days consecutively. They tied her to a table and placed a collar made of steel on her just like Cynthia, and made her undergo electric shocks and abused her with various sexual instruments. She was then transferred from the larger trailer to the smaller one and strapped to a chair; however she begged them to let her go.

They eventually did agree, and took her many miles away and eventually left her in the middle of a highway. Finally a police officer came along and he picked her up. Even though she reported it to the police, they didn't follow up on it, but with a case already against Ray she had a chance to get justice.

However now the media was raising a lot of questions as to why and how that report was not taken seriously and followed through on. In all honestly, no one realized how major an issue this was until now, and this was when investigators had finally taken this issue up with seriousness and were determined to get to the bottom of the entire ordeal.

The FBI started to send in profilers from their own units to help understand his psyche. Strangely, people who knew Ray always thought he was a pretty normal person, it was not until the police started uncovering all his secrets that the truth finally started to come out.

Cindy, Ray's accomplice eventually opened up about the abuse and torture they subjected their victims to and the details she provided were horrific. She had once admitted to a friend that Ray's ventures gave her a rush of adrenaline and that they had already killed at least 4 to 6 people.

To get rid of their bodies they dismembered them and threw the bodies into the nearby lake. They had learned to never submerge their victims whole as it is as they come up and do not remain under water. Thus, they would cut open their stomachs, to prevent the buildup of gases and the resurfacing of their discarded bodies.

She confessed that Ray had murdered about fourteen people at least, and gotten rid of the bodies in various lakes or ravines. In some instances he even had to undergo some questioning by law enforcement agencies but he always got away with it.

The main question that worried investigators was where the girl who they had seen being subjected to torture in Ray's video was. Due to the persistent news coverage, a woman came forward to the police and informed them that her son had recently married a woman who had gone missing for approximately three days and when she returned she had no recollection of where she had been.

They had assumed she was using drugs and had sent her away. However, luckily the police managed to find the woman except she hardly had any memories of what she had gone through. She however remembered Ray and some bits and pieces of the torture that she had been subjected to.

She remembered that she had been threatened and abused and then taken and dumped in the middle of nowhere but she could hardly remember what exactly she had gone through. While some may attribute this to post traumatic stress disorder, in reality Ray used to drug his victim so they would forget what they had gone through. He named the drugs in court that he used to induce amnesia in his victims, only further proving his conniving mindset.

David Parker Ray had many accomplices who took part in his activities. His own daughter was also witness to her father's perversions and sometimes even actively took part. Two or three other accomplices were also arrested with David and Cindy but finally his days of terrorizing women were over.

He went to trial and was sentenced to 224 years in prison for a number of different offenses and finally the killer ended up where he deserved.

Conclusion

The human race is quite a terrifying creation. While on one hand, we are capable of such great feats of kindness and goodness, the other end of the spectrum is all the more terrifying. The violence that can be demonstrated by the human race is not only worrisome but frightening.

For a seemingly normal person to commit these acts may seem ridiculous to most of us, but for years scientists and psychiatrists have tried studying exactly this, what exactly makes a person flip and turn into a cold blooded killer?

The inclinations of the human mind are quite difficult to understand, especially as to why some people can turn to such intense cruelty and disregard for the sanctity of human life. From the beginning of time mankind has been fascinated by those who manage to ignore all moral and social inhibitions and get lost in the madness that festers in their brains causing them to do these terrible things.

While the list of violent criminals is endless, some of them have made their place in history not just for their cruelty but also for their cunning. Thus, while their victims were subjected to horrifying deaths, we can only try and understand what it is like in the mind of a criminal and how they commit the crimes that they do against humanity...

Check Out My Other Books

Below you'll find some of my other popular books that are popular on Amazon and Kindle as well. You can visit my author page on Amazon to see other work done by me. (Brody Clayton).

True Murder Stories

Women Who Kill

Serial Killers

Cold Cases True Crime

Serial Killers – Volume 2

Cold Cases True Crime – Volume 2

True Crime

True Crime – Volume 2

True Crime – Volume 3

Serial Killers True Crime

Serial Killers True Crime – Volume 2

Serial Killers True Crime – Volume 3

LIBRARY BUGS BOOKS

Like FREE books?

Would you like them delivered to you every week?

Do you like non-fiction books on a huge range of different topics?

We send out FREE e-books every week so we can share our books with the world!

We have FREE books every week on AMAZON that we send to our email list. If you want in, then visit the link below to sign up and sit back and wait for new books to be sent straight to your inbox!

It couldn't be simpler!

www.LibraryBugs.com

If you want FREE books delivered straight to your inbox, then visit the link above and soon you'll be receiving a great list of FREE e-books every week!

Enjoy :)

www.ingramcontent.com/pod-product-compliance
Lightning Source LLC
Chambersburg PA
CBHW071259280526
45788CB00004B/1769